Urban-Chic Knitting Patterns for Fashion Dolls

An easy-to-make range of stylish
knitwear for 11-12" dolls

SUSAN DUNLOP

D1716954

Copyright

Urban-chic Knitting Patterns for Fashion Dolls: An easy-to-make range of stylish knitwear for 11-12" dolls
©2023 Susan Dunlop

Acknowledgements

Special thanks to the following small businesses, from whom I was able to buy realistic-looking miniature products, to create the settings for my dolls to show off their new knitwear.

Floral wall-art prints: downloadable to print at home, www.etsy.com/uk/shop/IsabelleSalemArt

Mini books: downloadable to print and assemble at home, www.etsy.com/uk/shop/MyPorchPrints

Newspapers: downloadable to print at home, www.etsy.com/uk/shop/DollStuffandmore

Coffee table: 1/6 scale handmade furniture, www.etsy.com/uk/shop/BozannaStore

Café table and chairs: 1/6 scale handmade furniture, www.etsy.com/uk/shop/SixthScaleStudio

Tea set and crockery: 1/6 scale custom tableware, www.etsy.com/uk/shop/ChikSculptures

Food items: 1/6 scale handmade food, www.etsy.com/uk/shop/katieannecraftsetsy

Shoes and boots: 1/6 scale footwear for fashion dolls, www.etsy.com/uk/shop/SindysWardrobe

Soft toys: miniature teddy bears and bunnies, www.etsy.com/uk/shop/KinsWonders

Fireplace: miniature dollhouse items to print at home, www.etsy.com/uk/shop/EasyPrintAndCut

OTHER PROPS: The settee, armchair, needle-felted pets, handbags and the craft room items, including the polymer clay sewing machine, ruler and rotary cutter are all made by myself.

Contents

Introduction

Following on from my previous book, *Modern Knitting Patterns for Fashion Dolls*, I've been busy designing this new collection of patterns, for you to have fun making, and for your dolls to enjoy wearing! Some of the projects include instructions for both slim-fit and curvy-fit finishes so they'll be more suitable for the different body shapes of vintage and modern fashion dolls. You can also make the sleeves and body lengths shorter or longer to suit your individual doll.

All the knitwear designs have step-by-step photos and easy-to-follow instructions, so that knitters of all skill levels can feel confident in achieving pleasing results.

If you're on Instagram, and you would like to share what you make, use the hashtags: #susieddesigns or #dollclothesbysusied, and also tag me, @susieddesigns, I'd love to see what you've been making!

I really hope you enjoy following the patterns in this book and that your dolls love wearing them!

Happy Knitting! Susan x

Knitting Tools and Supplies

Knitting needles – 2mm (US 0), 2.25mm (US 1) and 2.5mm (US 1½) sized needles are used for the projects. If you're looking for recommendation on which type to use, my favourite ones are KnitPro Karbonz Single Point Needles 25cm, which are carbon fibre with nickel-plated brass tips. The beauty of these is that they don't get all bent and misshapen with use!

Stitch holders – you'll need some small stitch holders, or you can use safety pins, which are my preferred option. I use two safety pins per set of sleeve stitches.

Stitch markers – you'll need four stitch markers for some of the designs, they need to be small for ease of using whilst knitting up the patterns. I like to use 5mm gold or silver jewellery-making jump rings. They don't get in the way while you knit and can be transferred easily from needle to needle. Stitch markers are used when knitting the raglan sleeve shaping so that you always know where the stitch increases are going to be.

Darning needle – a small, metal darning needle (wool needle) is used with matching yarn to sew up seams and to attach metal hook & eye fasteners.

Sewing needle and polyester threads – an ordinary small sewing needle and polyester thread are used for attaching buttons, sew-on poppers and lightweight zippers (which can be hand-sewn or machine-sewn).

Fasteners – you can use 5mm sew-on snap fasteners, narrow hook & loop, lightweight open-end zips, or size 0 hook & eye fasteners, for any of the jumpers or sweaters and 5-6mm buttons for the cardigans.

Yarn – The designs in this book use mostly 4ply (US fingering) yarn, as well as a few 5ply (sport weight) and DK (US light worsted or 8ply).

All the designs use smaller needle sizes than usual for the yarn weights, which makes the fabric look less bulky and more to scale on the dolls. Each design uses small amounts of wool so it's cost effective, meaning you could buy one ball of the pricier yarn if you wish or use up left-over yarns from your previous projects. I especially like to use Merino, Alpaca and Cashmere yarns as well as blends of these. They feel lovely to knit up and are so luxurious!

Abbreviations

K - knit stitches

P - purl stitches

st / sts - stitch / stitches

st-st - stocking stitch (US stockinette) knit right side rows, purl wrong side rows

g-st - garter stitch, knit all rows

1x1 rib (single rib) - [K1, P1] to end of row, repeat for each row as required

2x2 rib (double rib) - [K2, P2] to end of row, repeat for each row as required

yfwd (yarn forward or yarn over) - bring yarn between the needles, from back to front, then over right needle to knit next st/s as indicated, this will create a hole (for example buttonholes) and will increase work by one stitch

K2tog / P2tog (knit two together / purl two together) - knit or purl the next two stitches together, to decrease stitch count by one

kfb (knit front/back) - knit into the front loop and then the back loop of same stitch, before passing it over to the right needle, to increase by one stitch

M1 (make one stitch) - lift the bar between the stitches onto the left needle, by inserting the left needle under the bar, from front to back. Insert the right needle through the back of the new loop and knit to create a new stitch to then move across to the right needle. Continue with the pattern as instructed.

PM - place stitch marker, slip onto right needle before continuing as instructed

SM - stitch marker, slip over from left to right needle whenever you reach a stitch marker

BO - bind off / cast off stitches, basic casting off 'in knit' consists of knitting two stitches and passing the first stitch over the second and off the needle, knit another stitch, pass over last stitch and off needle, and so on… to bind off following pattern, this means if you've been knitting a 1x1 rib, then bind off would be: K1, P1, pass 1st stitch over the 2nd and off the needle, K1, pass previous stitch over and off, P1, pass previous stitch over and off, and so on…

Technique: attach a zipper

Use lightweight, open-end zippers, which are much easier to sew in place, rather than closed-end zips. Unless you can find them at very short lengths, just buy the longer ones, which can be trimmed to the required size as shown below.

With the zipper closed, pin both sides of the zip tape in place, with the zip pull positioned above the neck, alternatively use double-sided basting tape as shown here, it's a lot easier and no need to remove. Fully open the zip, then position the zip pull back up above the neck area.

Sew both sides of the zip in place, using a sewing machine with zip foot attached, or hand-sew securely in place. **Bring the zip pull back down to the bottom of the zip** before trimming the zip tapes at the collar. Use fray-check or textile glue to seal the cut end. Use matching yarn to over-sew new zip stops, between the top 2nd and 3rd zip teeth.

The Knitting Patterns

Classic Cardigan

This cardigan is simple yet stylish! It has a single rib collar, double rib cuffs and bottom hem, with front edging detail and small buttons. The buttonholes are worked into the pattern. This garment is knitted up in one piece, on the flat, from top down, with an increasing circular yoke for the shaping around the shoulders and sleeves. The only seams to join are the sleeves.

Finished size:

Length = 3.75"/9.5cm
Chest = 6"/15.25cm
Collar to cuff = 4"/10cm
Underarm to cuff = 2"/5cm
Gauge/tension: 40 stitches x 52 rows per 4" square, using stocking stitch, on 2mm needles

Supplies:

Yarn: 1 ball 4ply (US fingering) Example shown uses: West Yorkshire Spinners, Signature 4ply (available as 100g balls)
Needles: 2mm (US size 0)
Notions: stitch holders, darning needle, six 5-6mm buttons, sewing thread, needle

Classic Cardigan

PATTERN INSTRUCTIONS

Cast on 36 sts using the knit method,
1x1 rib for 6 rows

Cast on 3 sts, K to end of row (st count 39)
Cast on 3 sts, K3, P to last 3 sts, K3
(st count 42)

Buttonhole row:
K1, yfwd, K2tog, [K2, M1, K1] to last 3 sts, K3
(st count 54)
K3, P to last 3 sts, K3

K3, [K3, M1, K1] to last 3 sts, K3 (st count 66)
K3, P to last 3 sts, K3

K3, [K4, M1, K1] to last 3 sts, K3 (st count 78)
K3, P to last 3 sts, K3

K3, [K5, M1, K1] to last 3 sts, K3 (st count 90)
K3, P to last 3 sts, K3

Buttonhole row:
K1, yfwd, K2tog, [K6, M1, K1] to last 3 sts, K3
(st count 102)

K3, P to last 3 sts, K3
1st row = K
2nd row = K3, P to last 3 sts, K3
Repeat first and second rows, once each

Slip sleeve sts to holders:
K18, slip next 20 sts onto a holder, turn work to wrong side and cast on 3 sts, turn back to right side, (pull stitches together as you continue the row) K26

Slip next 20 sts onto a holder, turn work to wrong side and cast on 3 sts, turn back to right side, (pull stitches together as you continue the row) K18 (st count 68)

Classic Cardigan

Knit remaining main body as follows:
K3, P to last 3 sts, K3
Buttonhole row: K1, yfwd, K2tog, K to end
K3, P to last 3 sts, K3
1st row = K
2nd row = K3, P to last 3 sts, K3
Repeat first and second rows for 4 rows
Buttonhole row: K1, yfwd, K2tog, K to end
K3, P to last 3 sts, K3
Repeat first and second rows for 6 rows
Buttonhole row: K1, yfwd, K2tog, K to end
K3, P to last 3 sts, K3
Repeat first and second rows for 4 rows

RIB
K3, [K2, P2] to last 5 sts, K5
K3, [P2, K2] to last 5 sts, P2, K3
Buttonhole row: K1, yfwd, K2tog, [K2, P2] to last 5 sts, K5
K3, [P2, K2] to last 5 sts, P2, K3
BO main body sts following pattern

SLEEVES
Pick up one set of 20 on-hold stitches purl-wise, ensuring you'll be able to start with a knit row. Join yarn.

Cast on 2 sts, K to end (st count 22)
Cast on 2 sts, P to end (st count 24)

st-st for 22 rows

CUFF
2x2 rib for 4 rows
BO sleeve sts following pattern.

Repeat to make second sleeve

TO FINISH
Block/steam/press lightly to shape if required. Oversew the sleeve seams, then the underarm gap. Weave in loose ends of yarn and trim. Sew on small buttons, aligning them with the buttonholes.

Classic Cardigan

Slim-fit Polo-neck Jumper

This luxurious jumper is knitted in 5ply Alpaca yarn, for a gorgeously soft finish. It has a double-rib polo-neck, as well as double-rib cuffs and bottom hem. It has raglan sleeve shaping and is knitted up in one piece, on the flat, from top down. The only seams to join are the sleeves. An open-end zip or hook & eye fasteners can be used for the back closure.

Finished size:

Length = 4"/10cm

Chest = 5.5"/14cm

Collar to cuff = 3.5"/9cm

Underarm to cuff = 2.25"/5.75cm

Gauge/tension: 36 stitches x 48 rows per 4" square, using stocking stitch, on 2mm needles

Supplies:

Yarn: 1 ball 5ply (US sport) Example shown uses: Drops Alpaca 5ply yarn (available as 50g balls)

Needles: 2mm (US size 0)

Notions: darning needle, small stitch markers and stitch holders, hook & eye fasteners or open-end lightweight zip

Slim-fit Polo-neck Jumper

PATTERN INSTRUCTIONS

Cast on 32 sts using the knit method,

2x2 rib for 8 rows

K row

Raglan sleeve shaping begins

P7, PM, P4, PM, P10, PM, P4, PM, P7

K6, kfb, SM, kfb, K2, kfb, SM, kfb, K8, kfb, SM, kfb, K2, kfb, SM, kfb, K6 (st count 40)

P row

K7, kfb, SM, kfb, K4, kfb, SM, kfb, K10, kfb, SM, kfb, K4, kfb, SM, kfb, K7 (st count 48)

P row

K8, kfb, SM, kfb, K6, kfb, SM, kfb, K12, kfb, SM, kfb, K6, kfb, SM, kfb, K8 (st count 56)

P row

K9, kfb, SM, kfb, K8, kfb, SM, kfb, K14, kfb, SM, kfb, K8, kfb, SM, kfb, K9 (st count 64)

P row

K10, kfb, SM, kfb, K10, kfb, SM, kfb, K16, kfb, SM, kfb, K10, kfb, SM, kfb, K10 (st count 72)

P row

K11, kfb, SM, kfb, K12, kfb, SM, kfb, K18, kfb, SM, kfb, K12, kfb, SM, kfb, K11 (st count 80)

P row

K12, kfb, SM, kfb, K14, kfb, SM, kfb, K20, kfb, SM, kfb, K14, kfb, SM, kfb, K12 (st count 88)

P row

Raglan shaping ends, slip sleeve stitches to holders:

K14, slip next 18 sts onto a holder, turn work to wrong side and cast on 2 sts, turn back to right side, (pull stitches together as you continue the row) K24

Slim-fit Polo-neck Jumper

Slip next 18 sts onto a holder, turn work to wrong side and cast on 2 sts, turn back to right side, (pull stitches together as you continue the row) K14 (st count 56)

Knit remaining main body as follows:
P row
st-st for 18 rows

RIB
2x2 rib for 4 rows
BO main body sts following pattern

SLEEVES
Pick up one set of 18 on-hold stitches purl-wise, ensuring you'll be able to start with a knit row. Join yarn.

Cast on 2 sts, K to end (st count 20)
Cast on 2 sts, P to end (st count 22)
st-st for 22 rows

CUFF
1st row = [K2, P2] to last 2 sts, K2
2nd row = [P2, K2] to last 2 sts, P2

Repeat first and second rows once each

BO sleeve sts following pattern.

Repeat with other set of on-hold stitches to make second sleeve

TO FINISH
Block/steam/press lightly to shape if required. Oversew the sleeve seams, then the underarm gap. Weave in loose ends of yarn and trim. Sew on hook & eye fasteners for the back closure or use a lightweight, open-end zipper, which can be attached by hand-sewing or with a sewing machine.

Slim-fit Polo-neck Jumper

Curvy-fit Striped Polo-neck Jumper

This super-soft jumper is knitted in 5ply Alpaca yarn. The curvy finished fit is made slightly more generous, than the slim-fit polo-neck jumper, to suit curvy-body fashion dolls. It has a double-rib polo-neck, as well as double-rib cuffs and bottom hem. It has raglan sleeve shaping and is knitted up in one piece, on the flat, from top down. The only seams to join are the sleeves. An open-end zip or hook & eye fasteners can be used for the back closure.

Finished size:

Length = 4"/10cm
Chest = 6"/15.25cm
Collar to cuff = 4"/10cm
Underarm to cuff = 2.75"/7cm
Gauge/tension: 36 stitches x 48 rows per 4" square,
using stocking stitch, on 2mm needles

Supplies:

Yarn: two shades of 5ply (US sport)
Example shown uses: Drops Alpaca 5ply
yarn (available as 50g balls)
Needles: 2mm (US size 0)
Notions: darning needle, small stitch
markers and stitch holders, hook & eye
fasteners or open-end lightweight zip

Curvy-fit Striped Polo-neck Jumper

PATTERN INSTRUCTIONS

Cast on 32 sts, using the knit method, with pink yarn

2x2 rib for 8 rows
K row

Raglan Sleeve Shaping Begins
P7, PM, P4, PM, P10, PM, P4, PM, P7

K6, kfb, SM, kfb, K2, kfb, SM, kfb, K8, kfb, SM, kfb, K2, kfb, SM, kfb, K6 (st count 40)
P row

K7, kfb, SM, kfb, K4, kfb, SM, kfb, K10, kfb, SM, kfb, K4, kfb, SM, kfb, K7 (st count 48)
P row

Change yarn colour (light pink)
K8, kfb, SM, kfb, K6, kfb, SM, kfb, K12, kfb, SM, kfb, K6, kfb, SM, kfb, K8 (st count 56)
P row

K9, kfb, SM, kfb, K8, kfb, SM, kfb, K14, kfb, SM, kfb, K8, kfb, SM, kfb, K9 (st count 64)
P row

K10, kfb, SM, kfb, K10, kfb, SM, kfb, K16, kfb, SM, kfb, K10, kfb, SM, kfb, K10 (st count 72)
P row

Change yarn colour (pink)
K11, kfb, SM, kfb, K12, kfb, SM, kfb, K18, kfb, SM, kfb, K12, kfb, SM, kfb, K11 (st count 80)
P row

K12, kfb, SM, kfb, K14, kfb, SM, kfb, K20, kfb, SM, kfb, K14, kfb, SM, kfb, K12 (st count 88)
P row

K13, kfb, SM, kfb, K16, kfb, SM, kfb, K22, kfb, SM, kfb, K16, kfb, SM, kfb, K13 (st count 96)
P row

Curvy-fit Striped Polo-neck Jumper

Raglan shaping ends, slip sleeve sts to holders:

K15, slip next 20 sts onto a holder, turn work to wrong side and cast on 4 sts, turn back to right side, (pull stitches together as you continue the row) K26

Slip next 20 sts onto a holder, turn work to wrong side and cast on 4 sts, turn back to right side, (pull stitches together as you continue the row) K15 (st count 64)

Knit remaining main body as follows:

P row

st-st for 2 rows

Change yarn colour (light pink)

st-st for 6 rows

Change yarn colour (pink)

st-st for 2 rows

Change yarn colour (light pink)

st-st for 4 rows

Change yarn colour (pink)

st-st for 2 rows

Change yarn colour (light pink)

st-st for 2 rows

Change yarn colour (pink)

st-st for 2 rows

2x2 rib for 4 rows
BO main body sts following pattern

SLEEVES

Pick up one set of 20 on-hold stitches purl-wise, ensuring you'll be able to start with a knit row. Join with pink yarn.

Cast on 2 sts, K to end (st count 22)
Cast on 2 sts, P to end (st count 24)

Curvy-fit Striped Polo-neck Jumper

Change yarn colour (light pink)

st-st for 6 rows

Change yarn colour (pink)

st-st for 2 rows

Change yarn colour (light pink)

st-st for 4 rows

Change yarn colour (pink)

st-st for 2 rows

Change yarn colour (light pink)

st-st for 2 rows

Change yarn colour (pink)

st-st for 6 rows

Change yarn colour (light pink)

st-st for 2 rows

Change yarn colour (pink)

K row

RIB
2x2 rib for 4 rows
BO sleeve sts following pattern.

Repeat with other set of on-hold stitches to make second sleeve

TO FINISH
Block/steam/press lightly to shape if required.

Oversew the sleeve seams, then the underarm gap.

Weave in loose ends of yarn and trim.

Sew on hook & eye fasteners for the back closure.

Alternatively, use a lightweight, open-end zipper, which can be attached by hand-sewing or with a sewing machine.

Curvy-fit Striped Polo-neck Jumper

Slim-fit Long-line Cardigan

This stylish cardigan is knitted up in 4ply yarn. It has a single-rib big collar, as well as single-rib cuffs and double-rib bottom hem. It is knitted up in one piece, on the flat, from top down. It has an increasing circular yoke for the shaping around the shoulders and sleeves. The only seams to join are the sleeves. Small buttons are added to finish.

Finished size:

Length = 4"/10cm
Chest = 5.5"/14cm
Collar to cuff = 3.75"/9.5cm
Underarm to cuff = 2"/5cm
Gauge/tension: 40 stitches x 52 rows per 4" square,
using stocking stitch, on 2mm needles

Supplies:

Yarn: 1 ball 4ply (US fingering) Example
shown uses: West Yorkshire Spinners
Signature 4ply (available as 100g balls)
Needles: 2mm (US size 0)
Notions: stitch holders, darning needle,
five 5-6mm buttons, sewing needle, thread

Slim-fit Long-line Cardigan

PATTERN INSTRUCTIONS

Cast on 36 sts using the knit method,

1x1 rib for 12 rows

Cast on 3 sts, K to end of row (st count 39)
Cast on 3 sts, K3, P to last 3 sts, K3
(st count 42)

Buttonhole row:
K1, yfwd, K2tog, [K2, M1, K1] to last 3 sts, K3
(st count 54)
K3, P to last 3 sts, K3
K row
K3, P to last 3 sts, K3

K3, [K3, M1, K1] to last 3 sts, K3 (st count 66)
K3, P to last 3 sts, K3
K row
K3, P to last 3 sts, K3

K3, [K4, M1, K1] to last 3 sts, K3 (st count 78)
K3, P to last 3 sts, K3
K row
K3, P to last 3 sts, K3

Buttonhole row:
K1, yfwd, K2tog [K5, M1, K1] to last 3 sts, K3
(st count 90)
K3, P to last 3 sts, K3

Slip sleeve sts to holders:
K15, slip next 18 sts onto a holder, turn work to
wrong side and cast on 3 sts, turn back to right
side, (pull stitches together as you continue the
row) K24

Slip next 18 sts onto a holder, turn work to wrong
side and cast on 3 sts, turn back to right side,
(pull stitches together as you continue the row)
K15 (st count 60)

Slim-fit Long-line Cardigan

Knit remaining main body as follows:
1st row = K3, P to last 3 sts, K3
2nd row = K to end

Repeat first and second rows for 6 rows
K3, P to last 3 sts, K3

Buttonhole row: K1, yfwd, K2tog, K to end
Repeat first and second rows for 10 rows
K3, P to last 3 sts, K3

Buttonhole row: K1, yfwd, K2tog, K to end
Repeat first and second rows for 6 rows
K3, P to last 3 sts, K3

RIB
1st row = K3, [K2, P2] to last 5 sts, K5
2nd row = K3, [P2, K2] to last 5 sts, P2, K3
Repeat first and second rows once each
Buttonhole row:
K1, yfwd, K2tog, [K2, P2] to last 5 sts, K5
K3, [P2, K2] to last 5 sts, P2, K3
BO main body sts following pattern

SLEEVES
Pick up one set of 18 on-hold stitches purl-wise, ensuring you'll be able to start with a knit row. Join yarn.

Cast on 2 sts, K to end (st count 20)
Cast on 2 sts, P to end (st count 22)
st-st for 22 rows

CUFF
1x1 rib for 5 rows
BO sleeve sts following pattern.

Repeat with other set of on-hold stitches to make second sleeve

TO FINISH
Block/steam/press lightly to shape if required. Oversew the sleeve seams, then the underarm gap. Weave in loose ends of yarn and trim. Sew on buttons, aligning them to the buttonholes.

Slim-fit Long-line Cardigan

Men's Retro-style Cardigan

This retro-style, striped cardigan is knitted up in 4ply yarn. It has a single-rib big collar, as well as single-rib cuffs and double-rib bottom hem. It is knitted up in one piece, with raglan sleeve shaping, on the flat, from top down. The only seams to join are the sleeves. Small buttons are added to finish.

Finished size:

Length = 4.75"/12cm
Chest = 7"/18cm
Collar to cuff = 4.5"/11.5cm
Underarm to cuff = 3"/7.75cm
Gauge/tension: 36 stitches x 48 rows per 4" square, using stocking stitch, on 2.25mm needles

Supplies:

Yarn: three shades of 4ply (US fingering)
Example shown uses: West Yorkshire Spinners Signature 4ply (available as 100g balls)
Needles: 2.25mm (US size 1)
Notions: darning needle, small stitch markers and stitch holders, seven 5-6mm buttons, sewing needle and thread

Men's Retro-style Cardigan

PATTERN INSTRUCTIONS

Cast on 34 sts using the knit method, with grey yarn

1x1 rib for 10 rows

Cast on 3 sts, K to end (st count 37)

Cast on 3 sts, K3, P to last 3 sts, K3 (st count 40)

K row

Raglan sleeve shaping begins

K3, P8, PM, P4, PM, P10, PM, P4, PM, P8, K3

K10, kfb, SM, kfb, K2, kfb, SM, kfb, K8, kfb, SM, kfb, K2, kfb, SM, kfb, K10 (st count 48)

K3, P to last 3 sts, K3

Change to white yarn

Buttonhole row:

K11, kfb, SM, kfb, K4, kfb, SM, kfb, K10, kfb, SM, kfb, K4, kfb, SM, kfb, K9, **yfwd, K2tog** (st count 56)

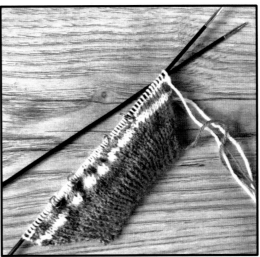

K3, P to last 3 sts, K3

Change to grey yarn

K12, kfb, SM, kfb, K6, kfb, SM, kfb, K12, kfb, SM, kfb, K6, kfb, SM, kfb, K12 (st count 64)

K3, P to last 3 sts, K3

Change to white yarn

K13, kfb, SM, kfb, K8, kfb, SM, kfb, K14, kfb, SM, kfb, K8, kfb, SM, kfb, K13 (st count 72)

K3, P to last 3 sts, K3

Change to black yarn

K14, kfb, SM, kfb, K10, kfb, SM, kfb, K16, kfb, SM, kfb, K10, kfb, SM, kfb, K14 (st count 80)

K3, P to last 3 sts, K3

Men's Retro-style Cardigan

Buttonhole row:

K15, kfb, SM, kfb, K12, kfb, SM, kfb, K18, kfb, SM, kfb, K12, kfb, SM, kfb, K13, **yfwd, K2tog** (st count 88)

K3, P to last 3 sts, K3

Change to white yarn

K16, kfb, SM, kfb, K14, kfb, SM, kfb, K20, kfb, SM, kfb, K14, kfb, SM, kfb, K16 (st count 96)

K3, P to last 3 sts, K3

Change to black yarn

K17, kfb, SM, kfb, K16, kfb, SM, kfb, K22, kfb, SM, kfb, K16, kfb, SM, kfb, K17 (st count 104)

K3, P to last 3 sts, K3

Raglan shaping ends, slip sleeve sts to holders:

K19, slip next 20 sts onto a holder, turn work to wrong side and cast on 3 sts, turn back to right side, (pull stitches together as you continue the row) K26

Slip next 20 sts onto a holder, turn work to wrong side and cast on 3 sts, turn back to right side, (pull stitches together as you continue the row) K19 (st count 70)

K3, P to last 3 sts, K3

Knit remaining main body as follows:

Knit the next 28 rows following the instructions in the table below, to change yarn colours when indicated and to make buttonholes on highlighted rows 1, 9, 17 and 25

1. **White yarn**, K to last 2 sts, yfwd, K2tog	8. K3, P to last 3 sts, K3	15. K row	22. K3, P to last 3 sts, K3
2. K3, P to last 3 sts, K3	9. K to last 2 sts, yfwd, K2tog	16. K3, P to last 3 sts, K3	23. **Grey yarn**, K row
3. **Grey yarn**, K row	10. K3, P to last 3 sts, K3	17. **White yarn**, K to last 2 sts, yfwd, K2tog	24. K3, P to last 3 sts, K3
4. K3, P to last 3 sts, K3	11. **White yarn**, K row	18. K3, P to last 3 sts, K3	25. K to last 2 sts, yfwd, K2tog
5. **White yarn**, K row	12. K3, P to last 3 sts, K3	19. **Grey yarn**, K row	26. K3, P to last 3 sts, K3
6. K3, P to last 3 sts, K3	13. **Black yarn**, K row	20. K3, P to last 3 sts, K3	27. K row
7. **Black yarn**, K row	14. K3, P to last 3 sts, K3	21. **White yarn**, K row	28. K3, P to last 3 sts, K3

RIB

K3, [2x2 rib] to last 3 sts, K3, for 6 rows, *making a buttonhole on 5th row = at last 2 sts:* **yfwd, K2tog**

BO stitches following pattern

SLEEVES

Pick up one set of 20 on-hold stitches purl-wise, ensuring you'll be able to start with a knit row on right side of work. **Join yarn using black yarn.**

Cast on 2 sts, K to end (st count 22)

Cast on 2 sts, P to end (st count 24)

st-st for 28 rows,
changing to white yarn for rows 17 & 18,
grey yarn for rows 19 & 20,
white yarn for rows 21 & 22,
grey yarn for rows 23-28.

Men's Retro-style Cardigan

CUFF

1x1 rib for 5 rows

BO stitches following the pattern

Repeat with other set of on-hold stitches to make the second sleeve

TO FINISH

Block/steam/press lightly to shape if required. Oversew the sleeve seams, then the underarm gaps. Weave in any other loose ends of yarn and trim. Sew on small buttons to align with the buttonholes.

Men's Retro-style Cardigan

Round-neck Flared Top: Slim or Curvy-fit

This retro-style, striped top is knitted in 4ply variegated yarn. It has a round neckline, and a shapely flared bodice, with picot edged hem and sleeves. It's knitted up in one piece, on the flat, from top down, with an increasing circular yoke for shaping around the shoulders. The only seams to join are the sleeves. Instructions are included for both the slim-fit and the curvy-fit version.

Finished size:

Length = 3.5-4"/9-10cm
Chest = 5-6"/12.75-15.25cm
Collar to cuff = 3.25"/8.25cm
Underarm to cuff = 2"/5cm
Gauge/tension: 36 stitches x 52 rows per 4" square,
using stocking stitch, on 2mm needles

Supplies:

Yarn: 1 ball 4ply yarn (US fingering)
Example shown uses: Lang Yarns Super
SOXX 4ply (available as 100g balls)
Needles: 2mm (US size 0)
Notions: stitch holders, darning needle,
open-end lightweight zip or hook & eye
fasteners

Round-neck Flared Top: Slim or Curvy-fit

PATTERN INSTRUCTIONS

START HERE FOR BOTH THE SLIM-FIT & CURVY-FIT VERSIONS

Cast on 32 sts using the knit method,
1x1 rib for 2 rows
K row
P row

Begin Shaping
[K3, M1, K1] to end of row (st count 40)
P row

[K4, M1, K1] to end of row (st count 48)
P row

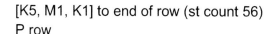

[K5, M1, K1] to end of row (st count 56)
P row

[K6, M1, K1] to end of row (st count 64)
P row

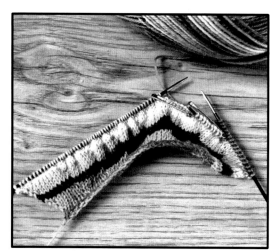

[K7, M1, K1] to end of row (st count 72)
P row

[K8, M1, K1] to end of row (st count 80)
P row

At this point, if you are making the curvy-fit version, follow on with the instructions on page 48. If you are making the slim-fit version continue here, as follows:

K row
P row

Shaping ends, slip sleeve sts to holders:
K13, slip next 16 sts onto a holder, turn work to wrong side and cast on 2 sts, turn back to right side, (pull stitches together as you continue the row) K22

Slip next 16 sts onto a holder, turn work to wrong side and cast on 2 sts, turn back to right side, (pull stitches together as you continue the row) K13 (st count 52)

Round-neck Flared Top: Slim or Curvy-fit

Knit remaining main body as follows:
P row
st-st for 14 rows
[K4, M1, K1] to last 2 sts, K2 (st count 62)
P row
[K5, M1, K1] to last 2 sts, K2 (st count 72)
P row
st-st for 4 rows

Picot edging to bind off
BO 2 sts [slip remaining stitch from right needle to left needle, cast on 2 sts in knit, BO 4 sts] repeat the steps within the brackets until you reach the last two stitches, BO remaining stitches.

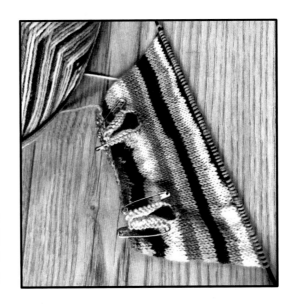

SLEEVES
Pick up one set of 16 on-hold stitches purl-wise, ensuring you'll be able to start with a knit row. Join yarn.

Cast on 2 sts, K to end (st count 18)
Cast on 2 sts, P to end (st count 20)
st-st for 22 rows

Picot edging to bind off
BO 2 sts [slip remaining stitch from right needle to left needle, cast on 2 sts in knit, BO 4 sts] repeat the steps within the brackets until you reach the last stitch, BO remaining stitch.

Repeat with other set of on-hold stitches to make second sleeve. *If you're using a self-striping yarn, try to start using the yarn at the same print section to achieve similar colours in each sleeve (most self-striping yarns repeat the colour change combination throughout the ball).*

TO FINISH
Block/steam/press lightly to shape if required. Oversew the sleeve seams, then the underarm gap. Weave in loose ends of yarn and trim. Sew on hook & eye fasteners for the back closure or use a lightweight, open-end zipper.

Round-neck Flared Top: Slim or Curvy-fit

PATTERN INSTRUCTIONS

CURVY-FIT VERSION
(continued from page 46)

[K9, M1, K1] to end of row (st count 88)
P row

K row
P row

Shaping ends, slip sleeve sts to holders:
K14, slip next 18 sts onto a holder, turn work to wrong side and cast on 2 sts, turn back to right side, (pull stitches together as you continue the row) K24
Slip next 18 sts onto a holder, turn work to wrong side and cast on 2 sts, turn back to right side, (pull stitches together as you continue the row) K14 (st count 56)

Knit remaining main body as follows:
P row
st-st for 12 rows
[K7, M1, K1] to end of row (st count 63)
P row
[K8, M1, K1] to end of row (st count 70)
P row
[K9, M1, K1] to end of row (st count 77)
P row
[K10, M1, K1] to end of row (st count 84)
P row
st-st for 4 rows

Picot edging to bind off
BO 2 sts [slip remaining stitch from right needle to left needle, cast on 2 sts in knit, BO 4 sts] repeat the steps within the brackets until you reach the last two stitches, BO remaining stitches.

SLEEVES
Pick up one set of 18 on-hold stitches purl-wise, so you can start with a knit row. Join yarn.
Cast on 3 sts, K to end (st count 21)
Cast on 3 sts, P to end (st count 24)
st-st for 22 rows

Picot edging to bind off: Same as instructions for slim-fit, see page 47

TO FINISH: Same as instructions for slim-fit, see page 47

Round-neck Flared Top: Slim or Curvy-fit

Men's Slim Polo-neck Jumper

This slim-fit, polo-neck jumper is knitted up in a variegated 4ply yarn. It has single-rib polo-neck, cuffs and bottom hem. It is knitted up in one piece, with raglan sleeve shaping, on the flat, from top down. The only seams to join are the sleeves. A lightweight, open-end zip can used for the back opening, or use hook & eye fasteners. This jumper can also be knitted in a plain yarn for a different look.

Finished size:

Length = 5"/12.75cm

Chest = 6"/15.25cm

Collar to cuff = 4.5"/11.5cm

Underarm to cuff = 3"/7.75cm

Gauge/tension: 36 stitches x 48 rows per 4" square, using stocking stitch, on 2.25mm needles

Supplies:

Yarn: 1 ball 4ply yarn (US fingering)

Example shown uses: West Yorkshire Spinners Signature 4ply (available as 100g balls)

Needles: 2.25mm (US size 1)

Notions: darning needle, small stitch markers and stitch holders, open-end lightweight zip or hook & eye fasteners

Men's Slim Polo-neck Jumper

PATTERN INSTRUCTIONS

Cast on 28 sts using the knit method

1x1 rib for 8 rows

K row

Begin raglan sleeve shaping

P6, PM, P4, PM, P8, PM, P4, PM, P6,

K5, kfb, SM, kfb, K2, kfb, SM, kfb, K6, kfb, SM, kfb, K2, kfb, SM, kfb, K5 (st count 36)

P row

K6, kfb, SM, kfb, K4, kfb, SM, kfb, K8, kfb, SM, kfb, K4, kfb, SM, kfb, K6 (st count 44)

P row

K7, kfb, SM, kfb, K6, kfb, SM, kfb, K10, kfb, SM, kfb, K6, kfb, SM, kfb, K7 (st count 52)

P row

K8, kfb, SM, kfb, K8, kfb, SM, kfb, K12, kfb, SM, kfb, K8, kfb, SM, kfb, K8 (st count 60)

P row,

K9, kfb, SM, kfb, K10, kfb, SM, kfb, K14, kfb, SM, kfb, K10, kfb, SM, kfb, K9 (st count 68)

P row

K10, kfb, SM, kfb, K12, kfb, SM, kfb, K16, kfb, SM, kfb, K12, kfb, SM, kfb, K10 (st count 76)

P row

K11, kfb, SM, kfb, K14, kfb, SM, kfb, K18, kfb, SM, kfb, K14, kfb, SM, kfb, K11 (st count 84)

P row

K12, kfb, SM, kfb, K16, kfb, SM, kfb, K20, kfb, SM, kfb, K16, kfb, SM, kfb, K12 (st count 92)

P row

K13, kfb, SM, kfb, K18, kfb, SM, kfb, K22, kfb, SM, kfb, K18, kfb, SM, kfb, K13 (st count 100)

P row

Men's Slim Polo-neck Jumper

Raglan shaping ends, slip sleeve sts to holders:

K15, slip next 22 sts onto a holder, turn work to wrong side and cast on 3 sts, turn back to right side, (pull stitches together as you continue the row) K26

Slip next 22 sts onto a holder, turn work to wrong side and cast on 3 sts, turn back to right side, (pull stitches together as you continue the row) K15 (st count 62)

P next row

Knit remaining main body as follows:

st-st for 26 rows

1x1 rib for 6 rows

BO stitches following pattern

SLEEVES

Pick up one set of 22 on-hold stitches purl-wise, ensuring you'll be able to start with a knit row on right side of work. Join yarn (note where in the variegated yarn print, you're joining, as you can start at the same print point to make the second sleeve match).

Cast on 2 sts, K to end (st count 24)

Cast on 2 sts, P to end (st count 26)

st-st for 28 rows

CUFF

K2tog, [P1, K1] x 3, P2tog, [K1, P1] x 3, K2tog, [P1, K1] x 3, P2tog (st count 22)

1x1 rib for 5 rows

BO stitches following the pattern

Repeat with other set of on-hold stitches to make the second sleeve, starting at the same yarn print point, if you are using variegated yarn, and you want to match the sleeve stripes.

Men's Slim Polo-neck Jumper

TO FINISH

Block/steam/press lightly to shape if required. Oversew the sleeve seams, then the underarm gaps. Weave in any other loose ends of yarn and trim. Attach your preferred closure, such as hook & eye sets or a lightweight open-end zip.

Men's Slim Polo-neck Jumper

40's Style Dress

This stylish dress is so versatile, it's great for everyday wear, yet smart and chic for any special outing! It has a round neckline, with elbow-length sleeves, and is shaped in at the waist. This dress is knitted up in one piece, on the flat, from top down. The only seams to join are the sleeves. A full-length zipper has been added for the back closure, alternatively use hook & eye fasteners or narrow hook & loop tape.

Finished size:

Length = 6"/15.25cm
Chest = 5"/12.75cm
Collar to cuff = 2.5"/6.25cm
Underarm to cuff = 0.75"/2cm
Gauge/tension: 40 stitches x 52 rows per 4" square, using stocking stitch, on 2mm needles

Supplies:

Yarn: 1 ball 4ply (US fingering) Example shown uses: West Yorkshire Spinners Signature 4ply (available as 100g balls)
Needles: 2mm (US size 0)
Notions: stitch holders, darning needle, open-end lightweight zip

40's Style Dress

PATTERN INSTRUCTIONS

Cast on 30 sts using the knit method

1x1 rib for 2 rows

Bodice shaping:

[K1, M1, K2] repeat to end of row (st count 40)

P row

K row

P row

[K2, M1, K2] repeat to end of row (st count 50)

P row

K row

P row

[K3, M1, K2] repeat to end of row (st count 60)

P row

K row

P row

[K4, M1, K2] repeat to end of row (st count 70)

P row

K row

P row

[K5, M1, K2] repeat to end of row (st count 80)

P row

K row

P row

[K6, M1, K2] repeat to end of row (st count 90)

P row

K row

P row

Separate the sleeve stitches onto holders:

K14, slip next 18 sts onto a holder, turn work to wrong side and cast on 3 sts, turn back to right side, (pull stitches together as you continue the row) K26

Slip next 18 sts onto a holder, turn work to wrong side and cast on 3 sts, turn back to right side, (pull stitches together as you continue the row) K14 (st count 60)

40's Style Dress

Knit remaining main body as follows:

P row

st-st for 2 rows

Waist shaping:

[K5, K2tog] x 4, K4, [K2tog, K5] x 4 (st count 52)

P row

[K4, K2tog] x 4, K4, [K2tog, K4] x 4 (st count 44)

P row

[K8, K2tog] x 2, K4 [K2tog, K8] x 2 (st count 40)

P row

Skirt shaping:

[K2, M1, K2] to end of row (st count 50)

P row

[K3, M1, K2] to end of row (st count 60)

P row

[K4, M1, K2] to end of row (st count 70)

P row

[K5, M1, K2] to end of row (st count 80)

P row

[K6, M1, K2] to end of row (st count 90)

P row

[K7, M1, K2] to end of row (st count 100)

P row

[K8, M1, K2] to end of row (st count 110)

P row

[K9, M1, K2] to end of row (st count 120)

P row

[K10, M1, K2] to end of row (st count 130)

P row

st-st for 20 rows

RIB

Option 1: 1x1 rib for 2 rows,
BO following the pattern

Option 2: g-st for 4 rows, BO in knit

40's Style Dress

SLEEVES

Pick up one set of 18 on-hold stitches purl-wise, ensuring you'll be able to start with a knit row on right side of work. Join yarn.

Cast on 2 sts, K to end of row (st count 20)
Cast on 2 sts, P to end of row (st count 22)

st-st for 6 rows

CUFF

g-st for 4 rows
BO in knit

Repeat to make the second sleeve.

TO FINISH

Block/steam/press lightly to shape. Oversew sleeve seams. Weave in loose ends of yarn and trim. Sew a lightweight, open-end zip or use narrow hook & loop tape.

Note: you can accessorise this dress with a belt, as shown here. Use a ready-made belt or make one, using a strip of scrap leather, with a tiny glued on metal buckle at the front, and a miniature (opening) belt-strap buckle at the back, so the belt can be easily taken on and off. You just thread through, fold over and glue each belt end to the belt buckle loops.

40's Style Dress

Faux Fur Coat: Slim or Curvy-fit

This super-chic coat is so soft and luxurious! Fluffy yarn is used to create a faux-fur style finish. It looks very realistic, and you don't see the stitches, so it looks just like faux-fur fabric. This coat is the ideal addition to your doll's eveningwear collection. It's knitted up in garter stitch, all in one piece, on the flat from top down with raglan sleeve shaping. The only seams to join are the sleeves. Instructions are included for both slim-fit (page 63) and curvy-fit (page 65) versions.

Finished size:

Length = 4-4.5"/10-11.5cm
Chest = 6.5-7"/16.5-17.75cm
Collar to cuff = 3.5-4"/9-10cm
Underarm to cuff = 2-2.25"/5-5.75cm
Gauge/tension: 28 stitches x 32 rows per 4" square,
using garter stitch, on 2.5mm needles

Supplies:

Yarn: 1 ball of fluffy yarn (with thin inner
core, like the yarn used in this example)
Example shown uses: Sirdar Snuggly
Snowflake chunky (available as 50g balls)
Needles: 2.5mm (US size 1.5)
Notions: darning needle, small stitch
markers and stitch holders

Faux Fur Coat: Slim or Curvy-fit

PATTERN INSTRUCTIONS

SLIM-FIT VERSION

COLLAR
Cast on 22 sts using the knit method
g-st for 6 rows

BEGIN RAGLAN SLEEVE SHAPING

K5, PM, K3, PM, K6, PM, K3, PM, K5

K4, kfb, SM, kfb, K1, kfb, SM, kfb, K4, kfb, SM, kfb, K1, kfb, SM, kfb, K4 (st count 30)

K row

K5, kfb, SM, kfb, K3, kfb, SM, kfb, K6, kfb, SM, kfb, K3, kfb, SM, kfb, K5 (st count 38)

K row

K6, kfb, SM, kfb, K5, kfb, SM, kfb, K8, kfb, SM, kfb, K5, kfb, SM, kfb, K6 (st count 46)

K row

K7, kfb, SM, kfb, K7, kfb, SM, kfb, K10, kfb, SM, kfb, K7, kfb, SM, kfb, K7 (st count 54)

K row

K8, kfb, SM, kfb, K9, kfb, SM, kfb, K12, kfb, SM, kfb, K9, kfb, SM, kfb, K8 (st count 62)

K row

K9, kfb, SM, kfb, K11, kfb, SM, kfb, K14, kfb, SM, kfb, K11, kfb, SM, kfb, K9 (st count 70)

K row

Raglan shaping ends, slip sleeve sts to holders:
K11, slip next 15 sts onto a holder,

Faux Fur Coat: Slim or Curvy-fit

Turn work to wrong side and cast on 2 sts, turn back to right side, (pull stitches together as you continue the row) K18

Slip next 15 sts onto a holder,
Turn work to wrong side and cast on 2 sts, turn back to right side, (pull stitches together as you continue the row) K11
(st count 44)

Knit main body as follows:
g-st for 30 rows
BO in knit

SLEEVES
Pick up one set of the on-hold sleeve stitches

Cast on 2 sts, K to end (st count 17)
Cast on 2 sts, K to end (st count 19)

g-st for 26 rows
BO in knit

Repeat with other set of on-hold stitches, to make the second sleeve

TO FINISH
Oversew the sleeve seams, then the underarm gap. Weave in loose ends of yarn and trim.

Faux Fur Coat: Slim or Curvy-fit

COLLAR

Cast on 30 sts using the knit method

g-st for 7 rows

BEGIN RAGLAN SLEEVE SHAPING

K7, PM, K4, PM, K8, PM, K4, PM, K7

K6, kfb, SM, kfb, K2, kfb, SM, kfb, K6, kfb, SM, kfb, K2, kfb, SM, kfb, K6 (st count 38)

K row

K7, kfb, SM, kfb, K4, kfb, SM, kfb, K8, kfb, SM, kfb, K4, kfb, SM, kfb, K7 (st count 46)

K row

K8, kfb, SM, kfb, K6, kfb, SM, kfb, K10, kfb, SM, kfb, K6, kfb, SM, kfb, K8 (st count 54)

K row

K9, kfb, SM, kfb, K8, kfb, SM, kfb, K12, kfb, SM, kfb, K8, kfb, SM, kfb, K9 (st count 62)

K row

K10, kfb, SM, kfb, K10, kfb, SM, kfb, K14, kfb, SM, kfb, K10, kfb, SM, kfb, K10 (st count 70)

K row

K11, kfb, SM, kfb, K12, kfb, SM, kfb, K16, kfb, SM, kfb, K12, kfb, SM, kfb, K11 (st count 78)

K row

K12, kfb, SM, kfb, K14, kfb, K1, SM, kfb, K18, kfb, SM, kfb, K14, kfb, SM, kfb, K12 (st count 86)

K row

Raglan shaping ends, slip sleeve sts to holders:

K14, slip next 18 sts onto a holder,

Turn work to wrong side and cast on 2 sts, turn back to right side, (pull stitches together as you continue the row) K22

Slip next 18 sts onto a holder,

Turn work to wrong side and cast on 2 sts, turn back to right side, (pull stitches together as you continue the row) K14

(st count 54)

Knit main body as follows:

g-st for 35 rows

BO in knit

SLEEVES

Pick up one set of the on-hold sleeve stitches

Cast on 2 sts, K to end (st count 20)

Cast on 2 sts, K to end (st count 22)

g-st for 30 rows

BO in knit

Repeat with other set of on-hold stitches, to make the second sleeve

TO FINISH

Oversew the sleeve seams, then the underarm gap. Weave in loose ends of yarn and trim.

Men's Variegated Jacket

This on-trend jacket is knitted up in 4ply sock yarn. It has a large, single-rib collar, as well as single-rib cuffs and double-rib bottom hem. It is knitted up in one piece, with raglan sleeve shaping, on the flat, from top down. The only seams to join are the sleeves. Small metallic buttons are added for a stylish finish. Variegated yarn gives this jacket such a stylish finish, your dolls will be so happy to have this classic garment in their collection!

Finished size:

Length = 4.75"/12cm
Chest = 7"/18cm
Collar to cuff = 4.5"/11.5cm
Underarm to cuff = 3"/7.75cm
Gauge/tension: 36 stitches x 48 rows per 4" square, using stocking stitch, on 2.25mm needles

Supplies:

Yarn: 1 ball 4ply yarn (US fingering)
Example shown uses: West Yorkshire Spinners Signature 4ply (available as 100g balls)
Needles: 2.25mm (US size 1)
Notions: darning needle, small stitch markers and stitch holders, seven 5-6mm buttons, sewing needle and thread

Men's Variegated Jacket

PATTERN INSTRUCTIONS

Cast on 34 sts using the knit method

1x1 rib for 10 rows

Cast on 3 sts, K to end (st count 37)

Cast on 3 sts, K3, P to last 3 sts, K3 (st count 40)

K row

Raglan sleeve shaping begins

K3, P8, PM, P4, PM, P10, PM, P4, PM, P8, K3

K10, kfb, SM, kfb, K2, kfb, SM, kfb, K8, kfb, SM, kfb, K2, kfb, SM, kfb, K10 (st count 48)

K3, P to last 3 sts, K3

Buttonhole row:

K11, kfb, SM, kfb, K4, kfb, SM, kfb, K10, kfb, SM, kfb, K4, kfb, SM, kfb, K9, **yfwd, K2tog** (st count 56)

K3, P to last 3 sts, K3

K12, kfb, SM, kfb, K6, kfb, SM, kfb, K12, kfb, SM, kfb, K6, kfb, SM, kfb, K12 (st count 64)

K3, P to last 3 sts, K3

K13, kfb, SM, kfb, K8, kfb, SM, kfb, K14, kfb, SM, kfb, K8, kfb, SM, kfb, K13 (st count 72)

K3, P to last 3 sts, K3

K14, kfb, SM, kfb, K10, kfb, SM, kfb, K16, kfb, SM, kfb, K10, kfb, SM, kfb, K14 (st count 80)

K3, P to last 3 sts, K3

Buttonhole row:

K15, kfb, SM, kfb, K12, kfb, SM, kfb, K18, kfb, SM, kfb, K12, kfb, SM, kfb, K13, **yfwd, K2tog**

(st count 88)

K3, P to last 3 sts, K3

K16, kfb, SM, kfb, K14, kfb, SM, kfb, K20, kfb, SM, kfb, K14, kfb, SM, kfb, K16 (st count 96)

K3, P to last 3 sts, K3

K17, kfb, SM, kfb, K16, kfb, SM, kfb, K22, kfb, SM, kfb, K16, kfb, SM, kfb, K17 (st count 104)

K3, P to last 3 sts, K3

Raglan shaping ends, slip sleeve sts to holders:

K19, slip next 20 sts onto a holder, turn work to wrong side and cast on 3 sts, turn back to right side, (pull stitches together as you continue the row) K26

Slip next 20 sts onto a holder, turn work to wrong side and cast on 3 sts, turn back to right side, (pull stitches together as you continue the row) K19 (st count 70)

K3, P to last 3 sts, K3

Knit remaining main body as follows:

st-st for 28 rows

RIB

K3, [2x2 rib] to last 3 sts, K3, for 6 rows, *making a buttonhole on 5th row = at last 2 sts:* **yfwd, K2tog**

BO stitches following pattern

Men's Variegated Jacket

SLEEVES

Pick up one set of 20 on-hold stitches purl-wise, ensuring you'll be able to start with a knit row on right side of work. Join yarn.

Cast on 2 sts, K to end (st count 22)

Cast on 2 sts, P to end (st count 24)

st-st for 28 rows

CUFF

1x1 rib for 5 rows

BO stitches following the pattern

Repeat with other set of on-hold stitches to make the second sleeve

TO FINISH

Block/steam/press lightly to shape if required. Oversew the sleeve seams, then the underarm gaps.

Weave in any other loose ends of yarn and trim. Sew on small buttons to align with the buttonholes.

Men's Variegated Jacket

Luxury Hooded Cape

This luxury, hooded cape is so chic! The hood is incorporated into the design, with an increasing yoke to shape the cape around the shoulders. It is knitted up in one piece, on the flat, from top down. There is just one seam to join, to finish the hood. Your dolls will love to wear this cape over their evening wear! You can make it any length to suit, short, mid-length or long, whatever you like! Use a clasp or hook & eye set for the neck closure.

Finished size:

Length = 4.75"/12cm
Shoulders circumference = 9"/23cm
Bottom hem circumference = 14"/35.5cm
Gauge/tension: 40 stitches x 52 rows per 4" square,
using stocking stitch, on 2mm needles

Supplies:

Yarn: 1 ball 4ply (US fingering) Example
shown uses: West Yorkshire Spinners,
Signature 4ply (available as 100g balls)
Needles: 2mm (US size 0)
Notions: darning needle, hook & eye
fastener or small metal clasp

Luxury Hooded Cape

PATTERN INSTRUCTIONS

Cast on 26 sts using the knit method,

HOOD
st-st for 2 rows

K5, M1, K5, M1, K6, M1, K5, M1, K5 (st count 30)
P row
K6, M1, K6, M1, K6, M1, K6, M1, K6 (st count 34)
P row
K7, M1, K7, M1, K6, M1, K7, M1, K7 (st count 38)
P row
K8, M1, K8, M1, K6, M1, K8, M1, K8 (st count 42)
P row

st-st for 30 rows

K2tog, K to last 2 sts, K2tog (st count 40)
P row
[K2, K2tog] x 5, [K2tog, K2] x 5 (st count 30)
P row

st-st for 2 rows

MAIN BODY
Cast on 3 sts, K to end of row (st count 33)
Cast on 3 sts, P to end of row (st count 36)

K3, [K2, M1, K1] to last 3 sts, K3 (st count 46)
P row

K3, [K3, M1, K1] to last 3 sts, K3 (st count 56)
P row

K3, [K4, M1, K1] to last 3 sts, K3 (st count 66)
P row

K3, [K5, M1, K1] to last 3 sts, K3 (st count 76)
P row

K3, [K6, M1, K1] to last 3 sts, K3 (st count 86)
P row

Luxury Hooded Cape

K3, [K7, M1, K1] to last 3 sts, K3 (st count 96)
P row

K3, [K8, M1, K1] to last 3 sts, K3 (st count 106)
P row

st-st for 40 rows

Eyelet and Picot hem

[K2, yfwd, K2tog] to last 2 sts, K2

P row

BO 2 sts [slip remaining stitch from right needle to left needle, cast on 2 sts in knit, BO 4 sts] repeat the steps within the brackets until you reach the last stitch, BO remaining stitch.

TO FINISH

Block/steam/press lightly to shape if required.

Fold the top edge of the hood in half, to form the hood shape, right sides together and oversew.

Weave in loose ends of yarn and trim.

Sew on a hook & eye fastener at the collar or attach a small button and sew a small yarn loop on the opposite side for fastening.

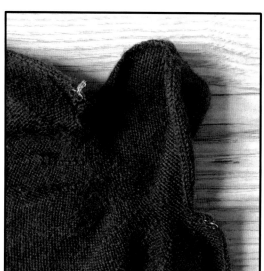

Luxury Hooded Cape

Zip-up Hooded Jacket

This zipped hoodie is so stylish! The hood is incorporated into the design, with the addition of functional pockets and a full zip closure. It has single-rib cuffs and bottom hem. The jacket is knitted up in one piece, on the flat from top down with an increasing circular yoke for shaping around shoulders. The only seams to join are the sleeves and pocket linings. Your dolls will want this one in their knitwear collection, for sure!

Finished size:

Length = 4.5"/11.5cm
Chest = 6"/15.25cm
Collar to cuff = 3.5"/9cm
Underarm to cuff = 2.25"/5.75cm
Gauge/tension: 40 stitches x 52 rows per 4" square, using stocking stitch, on 2mm needles

Supplies:

Yarn: 1 ball 4ply (US fingering) Example shown uses: West Yorkshire Spinners, Signature 4ply (available as 100g balls)
Needles: 2mm (US size 0)
Notions: stitch holders, darning needle, lightweight open-end zipper

Zip-up Hooded Jacket

PATTERN INSTRUCTIONS

Cast on 26 sts using the knit method,

HOOD

st-st for 2 rows

K5, M1, K5, M1, K6, M1, K5, M1, K5 (st count 30)
P row

K6, M1, K6, M1, K6, M1, K6, M1, K6 (st count 34)
P row

K7, M1, K7, M1, K6, M1, K7, M1, K7 (st count 38)
P row

K8, M1, K8, M1, K6, M1, K8, M1, K8 (st count 42)
P row

st-st for 30 rows

K2tog, K to last 2 sts, K2tog (st count 40)
P row

[K2, K2tog] x 5, [K2tog, K2] x 5 (st count 30)
P row

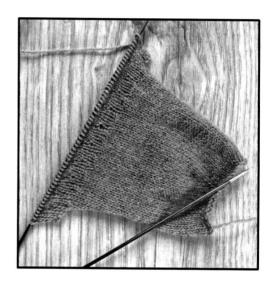

MAIN BODY

Cast on 3 sts, K to end of row (st count 33)
Cast on 3 sts, P to end of row (st count 36)

K3, [K2, M1, K1] to last 3 sts, K3 (st count 46)
P row

K3, [K3, M1, K1] to last 3 sts, K3 (st count 56)
P row

K3, [K4, M1, K1] to last 3 sts, K3 (st count 66)
P row

K3, [K5, M1, K1] to last 3 sts, K3 (st count 76)
P row

K3, [K6, M1, K1] to last 3 sts, K3 (st count 86)
P row

K3, [K7, M1, K1] to last 3 sts, K3 (st count 96)
P row

st-st for 2 rows

Zip-up Hooded Jacket

Slip sleeve sts to holders:

K15, slip next 20 sts onto a holder, turn work to wrong side and cast on 2 sts, turn back to right side, (pull stitches together as you continue the row) K26

Slip next 20 sts onto a holder, turn work to wrong side and cast on 2 sts, turn back to right side, (pull stitches together as you continue the row) K15 (st count 60)

Knit remaining main body as follows:

P row

st-st for 30 rows (*following instructions below to include pockets)

*on the 19th row = K6, slip next 6 sts onto a holder, turn work to wrong side and cast on 6 sts, turn back to right side, (pull stitches together as you continue the row) K36

Slip next 6 sts onto a holder, turn work to wrong side and cast on 6 sts, turn back to right side, (pull stitches together as you continue the row) K6, continue with following rows as before

RIB

1st row = K3, 1x1 rib to last 3 sts, K3
2nd row = P3, 1x1 rib to last 3 sts, P3
Repeat first and second rows for 4 rows
BO following the pattern

POCKETS

Pick up one set of 6 on-hold stitches, join yarn.
st-st for 10 rows
BO following the pattern

Zip-up Hooded Jacket

SLEEVES

Pick up one set of 20 on-hold stitches purl-wise, ensuring you'll be able to start with a knit row. Join yarn.

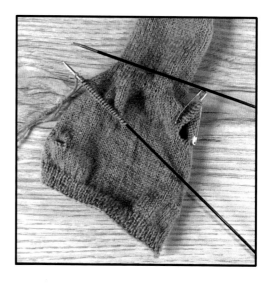

Cast on 2 sts, K to end (st count 22)

Cast on 2 sts, P to end (st count 24)

st-st for 22 rows

CUFF

1x1 rib for 5 rows

BO following the pattern

Repeat with other set of on-hold stitches to make second sleeve.

TO FINISH

- Block/steam/press lightly to shape if required. Oversew the sleeve seams, then the underarm gap. Weave in any loose ends of yarn and trim.

- Fold the top edge of the hood in half, to form the hood shape, right sides together and oversew.

- With the pocket flaps pushed through to the lining side of the jacket, oversew the side and bottom edges of each pocket to the inside of the jacket (ensuring the stitches don't show on the right side).

- Sew in a lightweight, open-end zipper, which can be attached by hand-sewing or with a sewing machine.

Cosy Winter Coat: Slim or Curvy-fit

This chic coat is so warm and cosy! It's knitted up in double-knit yarn on small needles. It has garter stitch collar, cuffs and bottom hem detail, with functional pockets. It's knitted up in one piece, on the flat, from top down with raglan sleeve shaping. The only seams to join are the sleeves and the pocket linings. Instructions are included for both the slim-fit and the curvy-fit version.

Finished size:

Length = 5-5.25"/12.75-13.25cm
Chest = 6-6.5"/15.25-16.5cm
Collar to cuff = 3.5-3.75"/9-9.5cm
Underarm to cuff = 2-2.25"/5-5.75cm
Gauge/tension: 32 stitches x 44 rows per 4" square, using stocking stitch, on 2mm needles

Supplies:

Yarn: 1 ball DK (light worsted / 8 ply), plus small amount of contrast shade. Example shown uses: West Yorkshire Spinners Illustrious DK (available as 100g balls)
Needles: 2mm (US size 0)
Notions: small stitch holders and stitch markers, darning needle, six-seven 5-6mm buttons, sewing needle and thread

Cosy Winter Coat: Slim or Curvy-fit

PATTERN INSTRUCTIONS

START HERE FOR BOTH THE SLIM-FIT & CURVY-FIT VERSION

COLLAR
Cast on 30 sts using the knit method, with **white yarn**
g-st for 5 rows
P row
Change to pink yarn, K row

BEGIN RAGLAN SLEEVE SHAPING

K3, P4, PM, P4, PM, P8, PM, P4, PM, P4, K3

K6, kfb, SM, kfb, K2, kfb, SM, kfb, K6, kfb, SM, kfb, K2, kfb, SM, kfb, K6 (st count 38)

K3, P to last 3 sts, K3

K7, kfb, SM, kfb, K4, kfb, SM, kfb, K8, kfb, SM, kfb, K4, kfb, SM, kfb, K7 (st count 46)

K3, P to last 3 sts, K3

K8, kfb, SM, kfb, K6, kfb, SM, kfb, K10, kfb, SM, kfb, K6, kfb, SM, kfb, K8 (st count 54)

K3, P to last 3 sts, K3

Buttonhole Row:
K9, kfb, SM, kfb, K8, kfb, SM, kfb, K12, kfb, SM, kfb, K8, kfb, SM, kfb, K7, **yfwd, k2tog** (st count 62)

K3, P to last 3 sts, K3

K10, kfb, SM, kfb, K10, kfb, SM, kfb, K14, kfb, SM, kfb, K10, kfb, SM, kfb, K10 (st count 70)

K3, P to last 3 sts, K3

K11, kfb, SM, kfb, K12, kfb, SM, kfb, K16, kfb, SM, kfb, K12, kfb, SM, kfb, K11 (st count 78)

K3, P to last 3 sts, K3

K12, kfb, SM, kfb, K14, kfb, SM, kfb, K18, kfb, SM, kfb, K14, kfb, SM, kfb, K12 (st count 86)

K3, P to last 3 sts, K3

At this point, if you are making the curvy-fit version, follow on with the instructions on page 91. If you are making the slim-fit version continue here, as follows:

Raglan shaping ends, slip sleeve sts to holders:

K14, slip next 18 sts onto a holder,
Turn work to wrong side and cast on 2 sts, turn back to right side, (pull stitches together as you continue the row) K22

Slip next 18 sts onto a holder,
Turn work to wrong side and cast on 2 sts, turn back to right side, (pull stitches together as you continue the row) K14
(st count 54)

Knit main body as follows:

K3, P to last 3 sts, K3

Buttonhole Row:
K to last 2 sts, **yfwd, k2tog**

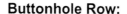

1st row = K3, P to last 3 sts, K3

1st row = K3, P to last 3 sts, K3
2nd row = K row
Repeat first and second rows for 4 rows

K3, P to last 3 sts, K3
K row
K3, P to last 3 sts, K3

Buttonhole Row:
K to last 2 sts, **yfwd, k2tog**

1st row = K3, P to last 3 sts, K3
2nd row = K row
Repeat first and second rows once each

Slip pocket stitches to holders:
K3, P3, slip next 6 sts onto a holder, turn work to right side and cast on 6 sts, turn back to wrong side, (pull stitches together as you continue) P30

Slip next 6 sts onto a holder, turn work to right side and cast on 6 sts, turn back to wrong side, (pull stitches together as you continue) P3, K3
(st count 54)

Cosy Winter Coat: Slim or Curvy-fit

Continue knitting main body as follows:
1st row = K6, K6, K30, K6, K6
2nd row = K3, P3, K6, P30, K6, P3, K3
Repeat first and second rows once each
Note: the highlighted stitches can be knitted in the contrast yarn as shown

Buttonhole Row: K to last 2 sts, **yfwd, k2tog**
1st row = K3, P to last 3 sts, K3
2nd row = K row
Repeat 1st and 2nd rows for 4 rows
K3, P to last 3 sts, K3
Buttonhole Row: K to last 2 sts, **yfwd, k2tog**
1st row = K3, P to last 3 sts, K3
2nd row = K row
Repeat 1st and 2nd rows for 4 rows
K3, P to last 3 sts, K3

RIB
Change to white yarn, g-st for 4 rows
(on 3rd row, K to last 2 sts, **yfwd, k2tog for buttonhole**)
BO in knit

POCKETS LINING
Pick up one set of the on-hold pocket stitches (6sts), **with pink yarn,** st-st for 8 rows, BO
Repeat with the other pocket stitches

SLEEVES
Pick up one set of the on-hold sleeve stitches (18 sts), **with pink yarn,** to start with a knit row.
Cast on 2 sts, K to end (st count 20)
Cast on 2 sts, P to end (st count 22)
st-st for 20 rows

CUFF
Change to white yarn, g-st for 4 rows
BO in knit, repeat with other sleeve stitches

TO FINISH
Block/steam/press lightly to shape. Oversew the sleeve seams, underarm gap and pocket lining. Weave in loose ends of yarn and trim. Sew on the buttons, aligning with buttonholes.

Cosy Winter Coat: Slim or Curvy-fit

Cosy Winter Coat: Slim or Curvy-fit

K13, kfb, SM, kfb, K16, kfb, SM, kfb, K20, kfb, SM, kfb, K16, kfb, SM, kfb, K13 (st count 94)

K3, P to last 3 sts, K3

Buttonhole Row:
K14, kfb, SM, kfb, K18, kfb, SM, kfb, K22, kfb, SM, kfb, K18, kfb, SM, kfb, K12, **yf, k2tog**
(st count 102)

K3, P to last 3 sts, K3

Raglan shaping ends, slip sleeve sts to holders:
K16, slip next 22 sts onto a holder,
turn work to wrong side and cast on 2 sts, turn back to right side,
(pull stitches together as you continue the row) K26

Slip next 22 sts onto a holder,
turn work to wrong side and cast on 2 sts,
turn back to right side, (pull stitches together as you continue) K16
(st count 62)

Knit main body as follows:
1st row = K3, P to last 3 sts, K3
2nd row = K row
Repeat 1st and 2nd rows once each
K3, P to last 3 sts, K3

Buttonhole Row: K to last 2 sts, **yf, k2tog**
1st row = K3, P to last 3 sts, K3
2nd row = K row
Repeat 1st and 2nd rows for 4 rows
K3, P to last 3 sts, K3

Buttonhole Row: K to last 2 sts, **yf, k2tog**

K3, P to last 3 sts, K3
K row

Slip pocket stitches to holders:
K3, P4, slip next 6 sts onto a holder, turn work to right side and cast on 6 sts, turn back to wrong side, (pull stitches together as you continue) P36

Slip next 6 sts onto a holder, turn work to right side and cast on 6 sts, turn back to wrong side, (pull stitches together as you continue) P4, K3 (st count 62)

Cosy Winter Coat: Slim or Curvy-fit

Continue knitting main body as follows:
1st row = K7, K6, K36, K6, K7
2nd row = K3, P4, P6, P36, P6, P4, K3
Repeat first and second rows once each

Note: the highlighted stitches can be knitted in the contrast yarn

Buttonhole Row: K to last 2 sts, **yf, k2tog**
1st row = K3, P to last 3 sts, K3
2nd row = K row
Repeat first and second rows for 4 rows

K3, P to last 3 sts, K3

Buttonhole Row: K to last 2 sts, **yf, k2tog**
1st row = K3, P to last 3 sts, K3
2nd row = K row
Repeat first and second rows once each

K3, P to last 3 sts, K3

RIB
Same as instructions for slim-fit version (p.89)

POCKETS LINING
Same as instructions for slim-fit version (p.89)

SLEEVES
Pick up one set of the on-hold sleeve stitches,
with pink yarn, to start with a knit row

Cast on 2 sts, K to end (st count 24)
Cast on 2 sts, P to end (st count 26)

st-st for 20 rows

CUFF
Same as instructions for slim-fit version (p.89)

TO FINISH
Same as instructions for slim-fit version (p.89)

Cosy Winter Coat: Slim or Curvy-fit

Cosy Winter Hat

This cosy hat is the perfect thing for a cold winter's day. It matches the cosy winter coat with its garter-stitch trim and pom-pom embellishment. It's knitted up in the same double-knit yarn, but you can use any DK yarn to match your doll's outfits.

Height = 1.75"/4.5cm

Circumference = 6.5"/16.5cm

Yarn: Small amount of DK (US light worsted / 8 ply), for the main hat, in shade of your choice, plus small amount of white/cream for the trim and pom-pom.

Example shown uses: West Yorkshire Spinners Illustrious DK (available as 100g balls)

Needles: 2mm (US size 0)

Notions: darning needle

PATTERN INSTRUCTIONS

Cast of 48 sts, in white yarn
g-st for 4 rows, change to pink/purple yarn
st-st for 8 rows

K2 [K2tog, K4] to last 4 sts, K2tog, K2
(st count 40)
P row

[K3, K2tog] to end of row (st count 32)
P row

[K2, K2tog] to end of row (st count 24)
P row

[K2, K2tog] to end of row (st count 18)
P row

[K2, K2tog] to last 2 sts, K2 (st count 14)
P row

[K2, K2tog] to last 2 sts, K2 (st count 11)

TO FINISH

Cut the yarn leaving a long tail. Thread the tail onto a darning needle and pick up the stitches purl-wise until they've all been transferred to the darning needle.

Pull the darning needle all the way through the stitches and pull on the yarn to gather up the stitches. Once tightly gathered up, secure by sewing with the darning needle.

Continue oversewing the side edges together, to make the hat shape.

Pom-Pom (optional)

Wind matching yarn around two fingers or cardboard, tie tightly and securely at the middle, then cut through the loops and trim to form a neat pom-pom shape. Sew securely to the hat.

Resources

The following shops are some of my favourite suppliers of yarn, tools and haberdashery:

West Yorkshire Spinners
http://www.wyspinners.com
UK based producers of British hand-knitting yarns. Manufacturers of Signature 4ply, Illustrious DK and many other gorgeous yarns!

LindeHobby
http://www.lindehobby.co.uk
Supplier of Drops Alpaca yarn as well as many other high-quality yarns. Very reasonable prices and shipping from Denmark.

Garnwelt
http://www.ebay.co.uk/str/diegarnwelt
German based supplier of Lang Yarns, including Super SOXX and other high-quality yarns. Reasonable prices and shipping through their eBay shop.

Love Crafts
http://www.lovecrafts.com
Suppliers of a wide variety of craft supplies, including a vast range of knitting tools, accessories and quality yarns at competitive prices. You'll find West Yorkshire Spinners, Sirdar and lots of other fantastic yarns here. Love Crafts also have some small fasteners, such as hook & eye sets, sew-on poppers and the KnitPro needles I like to use.

Etsy
http://www.etsy.com
There are a plenty of worldwide sellers, on Etsy, who supply small fasteners, including doll clothes buttons, tiny buckles and lightweight, open-end zippers.

Doll Clothes by SusieD
http://dollclothesbysusied.etsy.com
My Etsy shop, where I offer my range of sewing and knitting patterns for fashion dolls, play dolls and collectable, designer dolls. The patterns are available instantly, as downloadable PDFs, to print at home or view on your phone, tablet, laptop or PC.

Made in the USA
Columbia, SC
28 May 2023

17414626R00053